Let's Get Ready for School

JANE PORTER   CAROLINA RABEI

WALKER BOOKS
AND SUBSIDIARIES

LONDON · BOSTON · SYDNEY · AUCKLAND

A big change is coming...

Something amazing is about to happen. You're going to start **SCHOOL!** Are you excited? Nervous? Or maybe a little bit of both. These children know exactly how you feel.

Marley

Maya

Theo

Secretly, or even not-so-secretly, they are all a little bit worried too. Even your new teacher might be feeling a tiny bit nervous. It's only natural.

Akiko

Ella

Zakir

It's time to get ready

Whenever anyone starts a big adventure, it helps to be prepared. Athletes begin by stretching and touching their toes ... and you can warm up for school too. Can you do these things yet? (There's one that you won't need to do unless you're going to clown school!)

I can open a packet of crackers and almost peel a satsuma

I can wipe my own bum and I always wash my hands with soap after

I wish I could ride on a unicycle!

Some schools have uniform and some don't. What will you wear?

Why do I have to go to school?

School is for learning useful and interesting things – like how to spell elephant, why seeds grow, how many twos make four, and who lives at the South Pole. You might like spelling best or painting or running races – you don't have to love everything, everyone's different. All the things you learn at school will help you do exciting things when you're older.

elephant

$$2+2=$$

What would **YOU** like to do? It all starts at school...

I want to
be a space
traveller

I want to
write books
and poems

I'm looking
forward to numbers
— and trikes

Run, hop or scoot?

It's a good idea to practise getting to school before the big day. Make sure you leave plenty of time – the journey's more fun if you're not rushing. How are **YOU** going to get to school?

On the way home, you might stop for a treat or a trip to the library.

Walking is fun ...

and scooting!

I'd love to go by sledge!

Walking is the most fun because you can wave to all your friends on the way.

Time to say hello

It's time to take a deep breath, say goodbye to the person who takes you to school, count to three and ... say hello to some new faces! Who are you going to meet?

My cousin is at school already and my big brother

I don't know anyone

I've met the teacher already — they're nice!

But Daddy won't be there

It's OK if you cry a little bit when you say goodbye – it just means you are feeling a lot of love.

There might be animals ...

I hope there's a hamster

I wish there could be a class giraffe!

We're going to take turns to take Edgar Elephant home

and you'll meet your whole new class! In a few weeks, they will be as familiar as your own fingers and toes.

Our classroom

Now you'll get to know your special place for the year. Your teacher will show you where to sit and give you some pencils and books. Then they will explain where all the important things are – like the toilets. You will have your very own peg to hang your coat up.

There will be a carpet for listening time and a whiteboard to help with letters and numbers. There might even be yoga! At school, there will be special jobs to take turns with – like sticking the sun and rain on the weather chart.

TODAY

I think it's going to be sunny today

Will my picture be on the wall one day?

I love stretching like a cat in yoga

Time to talk, time to listen

At school, there are rules to help everybody to get along and learn. When your teacher is talking at school, it's time to be quiet. If you don't listen carefully, you might miss something really interesting.

Your teacher will ask questions, and if you think you know the answer, you can put your hand up.

I get it!

Ask me!

Me! Me! Me! I know!

It's not always easy to speak in front of everyone, but give it a try even if you're feeling shy and it should seem easier next time.

You will also need to learn all about taking turns and working as a team – especially when it's tidy-up time.

If you're not sure about something but don't want to ask in front of everyone, ask the teacher quietly later. Teachers LOVE to help!

Everyone's different

Just like grown-ups, children come in all colours, shapes and sizes. Some children in your class (maybe you?) might speak a different language – or even two – at home. And your new classmates will all have different personalities too – some loud, some quiet, some fun, some serious.

Sometimes children might be mean – but often it's because they are not feeling good about themselves.

Eating and playing

Halfway through the morning there will be snacks – maybe apples or bananas or pears. Then before you know it, it's lunchtime. Will you have school dinners or packed lunch?

I hope it's garlic bread today!

I like carrot sticks

I wonder what's in my packed lunch?

Sometimes there's an accident! But don't worry, there's always someone to help.

After lunch, it's playtime. There are lots of different things you can do. What will you choose?

When playtime is over, the teacher rings a bell. If you're lucky, the teacher might let you do it.

Will every day be the same?

No! There are lots of special days at school. There might even be "Golden Time". If everyone's done good listening and good learning all week, you get to choose what you want to do.

Then there are school special occasions ...

and fairs and plays...

Sometimes the whole class might go on an outing – to the library or swimming. You'll walk in pairs in a "crocodile", but don't worry – it doesn't bite!

The worry page

Everybody has some worries when they are starting something new – even grown-ups do. Ask your family what they can remember about **THEIR** first day at school – was it very different then?

What if I miss Mummy?

What if I don't like the food?

What if the teacher is very strict?

What if my babysitter misses me?

What if I get lost?

What if I get something wrong?

What if a parrot steals my sandwich?

What if no one will talk to me?

What if I cry?

If you're feeling worried, tell your family about it, even if it seems silly. Worries ALWAYS get smaller when you talk about them.

It's hometime!

At the end of the day there will probably be a snack and a hug waiting for you – and **LOTS** and **LOTS** of questions! All day your family have been wondering about **YOUR** day. You're lucky, because you **KNOW!** But what if you don't want to talk about it yet? Don't worry, it's normal to feel like that.

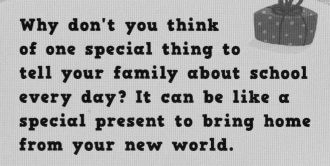

Why don't you think of one special thing to tell your family about school every day? It can be like a special present to bring home from your new world.

Was there a story?

Did you drink plenty of water?

What's the teacher like?

Akiko, Marley, Ella, Theo, Zakir and Maya – and **YOU** – are starting school soon. It's going to be scary and exciting and funny and interesting all at the same time. Good luck and enjoy your big adventure!